CHRISTIANITY: MYSTERY OF LOVE

AN ESSAY IN BIBLICAL THEOLOGY

by Thomas Barrosse, C.S.C.

FIDES PUBLISHERS, INC.
Notre Dame, Indiana

Imprimi Potest: Howard Kenna, C.S.C.,
Provincial

Nihil Obstat: Carroll Stuhlmueller, C.P.

Imprimatur: Leo A. Pursley, D.D.
Bishop of Fort Wayne-South Bend

By the same author: GOD SPEAKS TO MEN

Library of Congress Catalog Card Number: 64-23518

The ideas developed in this book were presented by the author somewhat differently and more briefly in the *Catholic Biblical Quarterly*, Vol. 20 (1958), pp. 137-172.

Manufactured in the United States of America

CONTENTS

THE PLACE OF LOVE IN THE OLD TESTAMENT CONCEPTION OF RELIGION

Christianity is a religion of love. To understand this oftenheard statement, we need only turn to the New Testament—*the* Christian book—and examine how its authors conceive of man's proper relation to God and note the place they assign to love in this conception. But in order to appreciate New Testament ideas, we must first turn to the Old Testament and consider briefly how its authors conceive of God and of man's relation to him and note the place love holds in this conception.

For the Old Testament writers, most clearly for those of the last 600 years before Christ, God is the all-transcending master of the world. He created it and, in particular, man. He directs the course of man's history, infallibly achieving his purposes. The anonymous prophet whom we call Second Isaiah, whose work, found in Isaiah 40-55, was composed shortly before 538 B.C., cites the God of Israel as declaring, "I am first, and I am last; besides me there is no god" (44:6), and again, "I am Yahweh, and there is no other. I form the light, and I create the dark. I produce peace, and I create evil. It is I, Yahweh, who do all these things" (45:6-7).

Yahweh and Israel. Among all the nations of men, however—and here the earlier writers are just as clear as the later—he chose, or "elected," one group as his very own. He revealed to Moses, their leader, his proper name, "Yahweh." By leading them across the Sea of Reeds he delivered, or "redeemed," a horde of Hebrews from enslavement to Egyptian overlords and the service of Egyptian gods. By covenanting with them at Mount Sinai he forged them into a "people of his very own." Election, redemption, covenanting—these were the three great divine acts which called the people of Israel into existence and gave them that unique relationship they enjoyed to the God of all mankind. Covenant—this was the peculiar kind of relationship they had with him.

By a covenant men of the ancient Near East did not merely exchange rights with one another as we do today by the modern contract; by a covenant they established a mutual relationship which enabled them to consider and to treat one another as members of one same family. By the Sinai covenant God, as it were, joined the family of Israel—or rather made them into a family which was his own. The terms most often used by Old Testament writers to describe the characteristic attitude and behavior of the God of Israel towards his people are the very terms that occur to describe the relationship of covenant-partner to covenant-partner or of family-member to family-member, especially of the stronger partner or member to the weaker. In Exodus 34:6 Yahweh uses these terms in describing himself to Moses. He declares himself "a God *tender* and *actively favoring,* slow to anger and rich in *loyal attachment* and *fidelity.*" "Loyal attachment" (in Hebrew, *hesed*) is the typical covenant attitude. "Fidelity" frequently accompanies it as a synonym. "Tenderness" and "active favor" specify how divine loyalty to the covenant most naturally shows itself.

If we are to have an accurate appreciation of Yahweh's relation to his people, it is important to emphasize that *hesed* does not mean mere observance of a contract. If by the Sinai covenant Yahweh joined the family of Israel, his *hesed* towards them was a warm family loyalty and, because it was divine, more lasting and reliable than any merely human family attachment. His tenderness towards his people was greater than any human tenderness—greater than a mother's for her child, as certain Old Testament passages point out. His active favor was ever at work, repeatedly helping his people in distress, readily pardoning the repentant sinner, and endlessly intervening on behalf of the defenseless and the exploited, especially the widow and the orphan. Yahweh's relationship to Israel, then, was by no means a cold juridical bond but a warm, active, and enduring personal attachment.

We would expect to find man's relationship to his divine covenant-partner designated as *hesed* too. Occasionally it is. The psalms, for example, frequently call the man who remains faithful to the covenant *hasid,* or loyally attached (to Yahweh or his law). But more often the faithful Israelite is said to *serve* his God whether through sacrifice and prayer (divine "service") or through observance of the terms of the covenant, the decalogue, by a "righteous" (or, as we often translate the word, "just") life. Also the faithful Israelite *fears* his God, that is, respects, reverences, and stands in awe of him. In the same way the gentiles and the unfaithful Israelites "served" and "feared" other gods.

The Old Testament looks not only upon apostasy but upon all sin as, effectively, a repudiation of the covenant. Most often Old Testament authors call it "rebellion" or "turning away," though they also quite frequently call it "depravity." The author of the great psalm of repentance, Psalm 51 (or, by the Greek Bible's numbering, Psalm 50), the *Miserere,* deftly contrasts the sinner's moral misery, described by these three terms, with the three characteristic divine traits. "Actively favor me, O God," he writes, "in accord with your loyal attachment; in accord with the abundance of your tender affection wipe out my rebellion. Thoroughly wash me from my depravity, and from my turning-away cleanse me."

A covenant-God who shows himself loyal, tender,

and actively favoring and a covenant-people that should be loyal, should serve and fear him but that often rebels, turns away, or commits depravity—thus does the Hebrew Old Testament conceive of divine-human relations. Love—at least the Hebrew word for love—is completely absent from this picture. Perhaps the reason lies in the use usually made of the term "love." Most often it describes the attraction a man experiences for a woman—strong, passionate, possessive. Of course, like the English word "love," the Hebrew word also designates other sorts of affection—fondness for things, friendship, parental love, and the like. But none of these kinds of affection have any particular relation to the notion of covenant—except, perhaps, that of friendship. Covenant-partners can certainly be called "friends." In fact, we do find Old Testament writers occasionally designating those who remain faithful to Yahweh as "Yahweh's friends," that is, his allies, those who are on his side. Translators often, though not quite accurately, render the expression as "those who love Yahweh."

We find two Old Testament books which explicitly describe as "love" the relationship between God and Israel: Hosea and Deuteronomy; and a few scattered later writers (for example, Second Isaiah) occasionally echo them. The background to this usage (at least in Hosea) may be the denunciation of Israel's repeated falls into idolatry as so many love affairs and the implied comparison of the covenant between

Yahweh and his people with the marriage bond (itself a covenant bond).

The prophet Hosea, or Osee, about 740 B.C. on the eve of the downfall and exile of the northern kingdom of Israel explicitly likens the relation between God and his people to a marriage. Israel, the wife, has proved disgustingly unfaithful. God must repudiate his partner—that is, send the people into exile. That, of course, terminates the covenant relationship. But all is not over. Probably in the light of his own persisting love for an unfaithful wife, the prophet has gained a deeper insight into the divine ways with men. Exile will not mark the end of divine good will. Something preceded and inspired the covenant: the election. The election-affection will outlast repudiation of the covenant and inspire its restoration. This election-affection the prophet calls "love." Like the attachment which preceded the marriage bond and which may continue to bind a man to a woman even after repudiation has severed the legally established bond between them, the immense divine good will towards the apostate people—the divine love—will outlast the expiration of the covenant bond and lead to its restoration.

Read the first two chapters of his book to see him develop the comparison. Then note how in 3:1 he describes his own persevering love for his unfaithful wife: "like Yahweh's love for the children of Israel," and how he goes on to explain that this love will bring the unfaithful partner back. Or see how in chapter 11, changing the figure from that of a husband to that of a father, he has Yahweh describe the election-affection which inspired the exodus and the covenant in these words, "When Israel was a child, I loved him, and out of Egypt I called my son" (verse 1).

As Hosea uses the term "love" to emphasize the immensity of the divine election-affection, so the book of Deuteronomy, cast in its present form perhaps a century after the prophet preached, employs it to underscore its gratuity. If Israel became Yahweh's people, it was only because he made them such. If he made them his people, it was not because they had done anything to deserve it but simply because he chose to do so. The book repeats over and over that Yahweh made them his people simply because he "loved" them and "chose" them. In 7:6-8, for example, we find Moses depicted as telling Israel: "Yahweh, your God, chose you to be a people uniquely his from all the peoples on the face of the land. Not because you were the most numerous of peoples did Yahweh become attached to you and choose you, for you were the least of all peoples. But out of love for you and because of the oath he had sworn to your fathers, Yahweh brought you out with a mighty hand and redeemed you from that place of slavery, from the power of Pharaoh, the king of Egypt."

Love freely given elicits a return of love. The book of Deuteronomy also speaks of the Israelites' love for God. It never suggests the sort of love that two equals might exchange: God's love and Israel's love are not mentioned together. For Deuteronomy, Israel's proper response to the gift of divine election is wholehearted observance of all of Yahweh's commands. But what better word than "love" to signify this total commitment of oneself and one's life to the election-God? Therefore, Israel must not only "fear" Yahweh (6:2), but Moses insists (6:4-5), "Listen, Israel: Yahweh is our God, Yahweh alone, and you must love Yahweh, your God, with your whole heart and your whole life and your whole strength," and he goes on to explain that this means keeping always in mind all his commandments, statutes, and prescriptions, ever obeying them, and teaching them to the coming generations.

Israelite and fellow Israelite. Man's relationship to his fellow man within the community of Israel is the result of the relationship of the community to Yahweh. The Israelites exist as a community—as a people—only because he made them such by his covenant. The terms of the covenant, the decalogue, regulate their relationship with one another. This relationship is most frequently called "righteousness," or—to render it as translators often do—"justice." The Old Testament term "righteousness" indicates behavior that befits a person. God is "righteous," or "just," when he protects the people of his covenant. Israelites are "righteous" when they live up to the terms of the covenant and in particular when they treat other members of the covenant-people as they should. This treatment certainly includes what our modern term "justice" designates. The prophets, for example, inveigh incessantly against the injustice of exploiting the poor and helpless—especially those typically defenseless ones, the widow and the orphan. But "righteousness" goes much further. It extends to care for the needier members of Israelite society even if this can only be done by almsgiving. In fact, by the end of the Old Testament period the word "righteousness" was the term regularly used to designate an alms.

Does love fit into this schema of the mutual relations of the covenant-people? The word serves to designate the relation of the Israelite to the other members of his people in a single Old Testament text, which is later echoed twice. Leviticus 19:17-18 condemns hatred (expressed in grudge-holding and vengeance) against a fellow Israelite and, in a contrast quite naturally suggested by this mention of hatred, prescribes, "You must love your neighbor as yourself." A few verses later (verse 34) the prescription is extended to include aliens resident within the Israelite community. Deuteronomy 10:19 repeats the latter passage. Interestingly, it motivates this "love" for the resident alien (verse 18) by pointing out that Yahweh himself is the resident foreigner's "friend" (or "lover") and support.

Old Testament law hardly ever concerns itself with the Israelite's relationship to foreigners (unless they become more or less permanent members of Israelite society). It treats apostate Israelites rather harshly. Certain Old Testament texts show a much less than cordial attitude towards foreigners. Others pronounce fearful curses against apostates and sinners. Foreigners and apostates are easily enough associated and all but identified if we note that the foreigners worshiped other gods and that apostates went over to this pagan worship. For a set of really fearful imprecations against sinners, see Psalm 109 (or 108 by the Greek numbering). Note also how the author of the book of Sirach, or Ecclesiasticus, less than two hundred years before the birth of Christ, urges discernment in almsgiving (12:4-6): "Give to the devout man," he says, "but do not help the sinner . . . , for the Most High himself despises [*literally,* hates] sinners and takes vengeance on the impious." He also expresses hostility for his gentile neighbors to the southeast, southwest, and north (50:25-26): "With two nations I am provoked, and the third is not even a nation: the inhabitants of the mountain of Seir and the Philistines and the stupid people dwelling in Shechem." If the Old Testament hardly even mentions love for fellow Israelites, it never even suggests such an attitude towards foreigners, let alone apostates.

Summary; the Greek Old Testament. Love, then, holds a place of rather minor importance in the Old Testament authors' conception of religion with the exception of two books, Hosea and Deuteronomy. These books use it not to replace the more generally accepted idea of the divine-human relationship (a very tender and vigorously active loyalty to the family-like covenant-bond on God's side and a deep reverence and generous compliance with their covenant-partner on the people's) but to nuance it: freely given and persisting divine benevolence towards Israel—Yahweh's "love"—antedates and underlies Yahweh's loyalty to the covenant, and the Israelite's fidelity must express itself in wholehearted commitment to Yahweh by generous observance of his law—Israel's "love."

When in the last two centuries before the birth of Christ the Hebrew Old Testament was translated into Greek, the influence of Deuteronomy's thought (and related later thinking) made itself felt. The gratuity of God's benevolence towards Israel became clear in the very terms the translators chose to render key Hebrew words. Rather than call the covenant-God "Yahweh," they rendered his name "the Lord." In the Greek Old Testament, then, he is Israel's Lord as he is Lord of all mankind. They used the word "testament" to render "covenant." The Greek Old Testament, therefore, speaks of a unilateral, freely given disposition of the Lord rather than of a bilateral agreement such as a covenant is. They also employed the term "mercy" to render "loyal attachment," "tender affection," and frequently also "active favor." The Greek Old Testament, therefore, speaks of the undeserved favor of a transcendent Lord rather than of covenant or family relations. Not that the Greek Old Testament presents God's relationship to Israel as any less warm and personal. In fact, several of the writings incorporated into the Greek Old Testament, although the Hebrew Bible lacks a Semitic version of them, contain quite vigorous underscorings of its warmth and tenderness. Nor that the translators lost sight of the importance of the exodus from Egypt and the events at Sinai—they simply viewed them from a vantage point somewhat different from that of the earlier authors of the Hebrew Bible. They perceived and expressed more emphatically the transcendence of the God who had made Israel a people and the gratuity of the favor he had thereby done them. This emphasis on freely given election led them to render Hebrew designations for Israel which they did not understand (such as "Yeshurun" in Deuteronomy 33:5 and elsewhere) by the term "love," since in the Hebrew Old Testament divine love was Yahweh's gratuitous election-affection. Hence, in the Greek Old Testament, "love" occurs in a religious sense more often than in the Hebrew Bible, but the extra instances are almost always occurrences of the expression "the Lord's beloved," that is, the Lord's elect or chosen.

A final note of interest regarding the Greek Old Testament is the Greek term the translators chose to render the Hebrew word for love. Greek is a rich language. It has several terms for love: *storgē* (family love), *érōs* (passionate, possessive love), *philía* (friendship or tender affection), and *agápē* (respectful, preferential love). The second and third of these four were the most commonly used terms in the earlier, classical period and in the language spoken at the time the Hebrew Bible was translated into Greek. Probably because God's love is preferential election-love, the translators employed the last of the four for almost every occurrence of love in a religious sense. The New Testament authors followed this usage. There are only two exceptions. In compound words such as the adjectives "money-loving" and "pleasure-loving" and the noun "love-for-men" (*philanthrōpía*), the third of the four had to be used —since it is the only one of the four that regularly forms compounds. In the Johannine writings the derivatives of *philía* occur with some frequency to designate a particularly warm affection. To distinguish this Greek term from the more common *agápē*, we can render it "cherish" (or, if it occurs in noun form, "friend" or "friendship").

THE NEW TESTAMENT CONCEPTION OF RELIGION

Father, Son, Spirit. The New Testament conception of the divine-human relationship differs from the Old Testament's. Jesus, of course, was a Jew. He spoke of the God of Moses as his own God. But if we may judge from the Gospel records, he did not call him "Yahweh" ("the Lord") except in quoting Old Testament passages that used this divine title. Though he referred to him often as "God," he preferred to call him "Father." Nor was this merely a pretty metaphor. God was Jesus' Father in an altogether unique sense. God was simply "*the* Father" and Jesus was "*the* Son" (for example, in Matthew 11:27). Jesus addressed him in prayer with the very Aramaic expression that a child employed with its own male parent: "Abba" (Mark 14:36).

While always distinguishing himself from God his Father (who remains the *only* God—see Mark 12:29) and yet at the same time acting like God (pardoning sins, working miracles, modifying the divine law of the Old Testament, and in all of these instances acting on his own authority and not simply as one sent by God), he reveals his identity as Son of God made man—truly man but also truly Son: Son in the proper and literal sense of the word. In this way he revealed the mystery of the intimate life of God: the fact that God is a Father and has a Son in the strictest sense of the terms.

The fatherhood of God in this New Testament sense (like the existence of a divine Son in this New Testament sense) is not to be found before the advent of Christianity. Although God was sometimes called father in a literal sense, such a manner of speaking among pagan peoples often had as its basis a crude and materialistic concept of God: real paternity but not of a true God. Ordinarily divine paternity was understood in a purely metaphorical sense. God was father in that he was creator, therefore the father of all: of men *and of things*. Or he was father in that he was good, benevolent, and paternal *like* a father. For Old Testament Israel he was father of his people in that he had "created" them as a people (see, for example, Malachi 2:10)—but Old Testament use of the idea is relatively infrequent.

Jesus did not declare God the Father of all men or even of all Israel. He was the Father of Jesus himself and of all those who became Jesus' disciples. Of course, he made it clear that discipleship was open to all men, even non-Jews; indeed, it was incumbent upon all to become his disciples. But only those who became disciples could share Jesus' filial relationship to God.

Jesus came not merely to announce that God was Father but to make divine paternity a reality for men. Hence, he appears from the beginning of his ministry as a messenger of salvation—as a prophet, as the "son of man" (in Daniel 7), and finally as the Christ or messiah. He invites all men to join with him to enjoy the salvation he announces (or, more precisely, to enjoy the reign of God over their lives). Gradually it grows clearer to those who comply that to accept discipleship means not only to share his life but to share his relationship to God. When they finally realize that he is Son of God, they realize that they share in the relations of the Son with the Father and that in this sharing lies the salvation which he offers.

In the New Testament God is never called Father merely to signify that he is fatherly. He is called simply *the* Father (often with a direct allusion to his relation to his only Son as in Matthew 11:27). Or Jesus calls him *his* Father (Matthew 11:25-27). He is also called Father by the disciples, truly his sons because they alone are the true brothers of Jesus (Matthew 12:48-50). Though he wants to be Father of all men, he does not become such until men accept discipleship. To be a son of God, Saints Paul and John point out, one must be born of God by a second birth entirely distinct from creation (Titus 3:5; John 3:3-6). The new birth gives a man a new life, eternal life or life of the age to come, which comes from God (Romans 5:17-21; 6:11; John 3:15-16).

In Jesus' time Judaism was awaiting an outpouring of the transforming divine power, or "spirit." The event was to happen when the long-expected divine salvation. He himself had this divine, or holy, spirit, the instrument by which God would work that divine salvation. He himself had this divine, or holy spirit, and he promised and gave it to his disciples. It was this spirit—or we may write "Spirit" because the Spirit happens to be a person—that would make the disciples one with Jesus and enable them to share his relations with God.

Saint Paul says all this succinctly in his letter to the Galatian Christians (Galatians 4:4-6). "When the appointed time came," he writes, "God sent his Son . . . that we might receive adoption as sons. And the proof that you are sons? God has sent the Spirit of his Son into our hearts with the cry, 'Abba (Father)!'" Or again, writing to the Christians of Rome (Romans 8:14-15), he explains, "Those who are led by God's Spirit are God's sons. You have not received once again [as Israel did] a spirit of service to inspire fear [the two important Old Testament words for man's attitude towards God], but you have received a spirit of filial adoption, in which we cry out, 'Abba (Father)!'" The New Testament conception of the divine-human relationship is, therefore, a father-son relationship in which Jesus is the

Son and all those who by reception of his Spirit become one with him share in his sonship.

Being sons. The filial status man enjoys imposes on him the duty of imitating his heavenly Father. "You must be perfect," Jesus tells his disciples (Matthew 5:48), "as your heavenly Father is perfect." This new status of sonship, in which man imitates God, is synonymous with the awaited kingdom—or reign—of God over men's lives; it is synonymous with sharing in the new life, the "everlasting life"—or, more accurately, the life of the age to come—desired by many of Jesus' contemporaries.

A single obstacle stands in the way of this sonship or reign or life: sin. The term most often used in the New Testament to designate it, a term taken from the Old Testament and the one which we usually translate into English as "sin," means quite literally "turning away" or "missing the mark." When we later examine the New Testament passages that speak of it, we shall find that it turns out to be not merely a turning away from God or Jesus but a possessive clinging to what we would have to give up in order to live the kind of life Jesus demands. In short, it is selfishness. For this reason, Jesus insists that his followers must be ready to "deny"—that is, to say no to—themselves, to "lose" and even "despise" all things, including their very lives, in order to be his disciples.

The first move away from a self-centered existence

is "repentance," a word which literally means a change of heart. Jesus begins his ministry in the Gospels of Matthew (4:17) and Mark (1:15) with the demand, "Repent for the kingdom [*or* reign] of God is at hand": men must repent if God is to reign over their lives. But in the Markan Gospel Jesus makes clear that this repentance is no mere turning away from selfishness. It is positive. Men, he says, must "repent *and believe* in the good news" he preaches (Mark 1:15). He demands not only a turning from self but at the same time a turning to God who is revealing himself—who is offering men a new relationship to himself. Faith means accepting that offer, saying yes to God's self-revelation in Jesus; it means a man's effective commitment of himself to Jesus so as to share his filial relationship with the Father.

Repentance is the condition and faith the first step to union with Jesus—a union that assures a man of having Jesus' Spirit and therefore of sharing in Jesus' sonship. Self-denial, readiness to "lose" oneself, is the condition and imitating the Father the way of maintaining one's union with Jesus. But all this does not make the union complete. Full union or sharing with Jesus will come only after death at the resurrection which accompanies the final judgment. Therefore the disciples spend their earthly lives in hope.

The whole picture, glorious as it may look, has its

painful implications. The initial repentance, the enduring self-denial, and the final self-renunciation of death all suggest difficulty and suffering. In fact, in a saying found in each of the first three Gospels Jesus compares the life of his disciples to a cross-carrying, alluding to the Roman practice of having condemned criminals carry to the place of execution the instrument on which they were to die. Even more, Jesus insists that his own life will end very literally in a cross-carrying and death on a cross, to be followed by resurrection to a glorious new existence. He insists that he must die in this way in order to rise, that this utter self-renunciation of his passion is a necessary condition for his entering into glory, and indeed that it is the necessary condition for his disciples' self-renunciation to have any efficacy. Their initial repentance, enduring self-denial, and final self-renunciation in death will bring them effectively into union with God only if this effort of theirs is a sharing in his cross. The new status or life that comes to them with faith, its development as they live in imitation of the heavenly Father, and its fullness at the final resurrection are all really a sharing in the glory he has as a result of the total self-renunciation of his cross.

God, then, is Father. Jesus is Son. Men who accept him with repentance and by faith receive his Spirit and so share in his sonship. They live in imitation of their Father at the cost of continued self-denial. They wait in hope for the final fullness of sonship, which will come with resurrection after the final self-renunciation of death. The cross and resurrection of Jesus are what give efficacy to the disciples' self-renunciation and commitment to God.

Man and fellow man. What is the relationship of man to man in this conception? If God is Father and men are sons, then they are brothers to one another. Indeed, in the Acts of the Apostles right after Pentecost the disciples refer to themselves as "the brothers." If the community of disciples simply shares in Jesus' sonship, then they may also look upon and treat one another as being in some sense Jesus. In fact, in the parable of the Last Judgment (Matthew 25:31-46), Jesus declares good done to the least of his "brothers" good done to himself. If a share in his sonship is meant for *all* men, then they can all be looked upon in this way—as at least potentially brothers or in some sense Jesus himself.

Where does love fit into this picture? We have completely avoided the term so far but not because New Testament writers avoid it. In fact, they use it with extraordinary frequency (319 times) and interpret this entire schema of the divine-human relationship in terms of love. But for clarity's sake we have tried to look at the schema first. Now let us examine its interpretation in terms of love by each of the major New Testament writings. First, we shall examine briefly how the more important New Testament authors use the Greek word for love in explaining God's plan of salvation in Christ. Then we shall try to see how it may be used to understand even those aspects of their exposition which they themselves do not present clearly in terms of love.

LOVE IN THE SYNOPTIC GOSPELS

The first three Gospels—called "Synoptic" because they give more or less the *same view* of the gospel story—do not use the term "love" so frequently as the fourth Gospel or the Pauline epistles. But all three use it in key passages—Luke more often than Mark, however, and Matthew more often than Luke.

God and Jesus. In the Synoptic Gospels Jesus describes God as Father—his own Father first of all. To say "father," of course, is to say "love," and this is true, above all, of the heavenly Father's relation to his Son Jesus. Jesus appears as his "beloved" Son in three very important texts.

At the moment when Jesus begins his public ministry, just after his baptism by John (Matthew 3:16-17; Mark 1:10-11; Luke 3:21-22), the Savior sees the heavens opened and the divine Spirit come down upon him to guide him in his saving work and hears God's voice call out from above: "You are my beloved Son; in you I take my delight." (In Matthew the voice speaks rather to John the Baptist or to the bystanders: "This is my beloved Son, in whom I take my delight.") Commentators see in the divine words references to at least two important Old Testament texts: Isaiah 42:1 (in which God speaks of his chosen servant, teacher of his law, in whom he delights and upon whom he sends his spirit) and Psalm 2:7 (in which the Davidic king cites Yahweh's words to him: "You are my son"). The divine words spoken at his baptism, then, identify Jesus with two of the great Old Testament savior-figures: the servant of the Lord from the book of Isaiah and the Davidic messiah. Neither of these texts, however, contains the word "beloved." When the expression occurs of a son in the Old Testament, it regularly refers to an *only* son, all the dearer to his parents for being their only. By this word, then, the divine voice identifies Jesus as God's Son in a unique sense of the word while also characterizing God's paternal relationship to him as basically one of love.

At the transfiguration (Matthew 17:1-8; Mark 9:2-8; Luke 9:28-36), that moment during the public ministry when Jesus' identity shines out most clearly to the three Apostles chosen to witness the event, the Father once more characterizes his relationship to Jesus as love. The Apostles see their master transfigured with glory. They sense the divine presence when the cloud settles down over them as the cloud signifying the divine presence during the days of Israel's desert wanderings settled down over the tabernacle, or tent, set up by Moses to show that God was taking possession of his abode among men. They hear the divine voice, "This is my beloved [*in Luke*:

my chosen] Son [*Matthew adds*: in whom I take my delight]; listen to him." Commentators see in the divine words references to the same Old Testament texts as above and in the addition, "listen to him," a reference to Moses' declaration in Deuteronomy 18:15-19 that God would later raise up for the Israelites a prophet like himself to whom they must listen. God would, then, be identifying Jesus as the chosen servant of the Lord, the messianic king, and the promised prophet of whom the Old Testament speaks. But at this moment when Jesus' glory shines out most clearly, God would be identifying him especially as his Son in an altogether unique sense: "beloved"—only—Son, and describing his paternal relationship to him in terms of love.

Finally, in the parable of the Wicked Vinedressers (Matthew 21:33-46; Mark 12:1-12; Luke 20:9-19), as his passion draws near, Jesus threatens the authorities hostile to him with rejection by God for their rejection of him. In castigating them, he depicts their reaction to him as very like their reaction to the other divine emissaries to Israel who preceded him. But he contrasts himself with his predecessors: they were only the vineyard owner's "slaves," while he, coming last of all and in Mark as the only one left, is the "son"—in Mark and Luke, "beloved son." Rejection of God's only and beloved Son by them assures their being rejected by God.

God and Jesus' disciples. The Synoptic Gospels

nowhere speak of the Father's love for Jesus' disciples. Of course, the disciples share in Jesus' relation to the Father. It seems quite justifiable to conclude that they are objects of the Father's love for him. Indeed, God's care for the disciples, as the Gospels depict it, can hardly be described as anything but paternal and loving. Their heavenly Father, Jesus says, will provide them with food more surely than he provides for the wild birds; he will provide them with clothing more surely than he provides for the wild flowers (Matthew 6:25-34). He knows how to give good things to those who ask him much better than any human father knows how to give good things to his child (Matthew 7:11). Though in the Synoptics Jesus never calls this kindly care love, he does propose it as model for his disciples' love; by imitating the goodness (Luke calls it "kindness") which the Father shows even for sinners in offering them his rain and his sunlight, they fulfill Jesus' command to love. Perhaps the term "love"—apart from the last text mentioned—does not occur on Jesus' lips to describe God's relationship to men because the word "father" suffices to imply it and says even more than "love" would alone.

Since God reveals himself in and through Jesus, we cannot go amiss if we conclude to God's attitude towards men from Jesus' own. Peter's description of the public ministry given to the Roman Cornelius' household in Acts 10:38 accurately summarizes the Synoptic ministry account: "He went about *doing good* and healing all who were oppressed by the devil because God was with him." The evangelists describe him several times over as "moved with compassion" at the needs of the people—as he is, for example, before he sends his apostles out to preach to the shepherdless masses in Matthew 9:36. They depict the needy begging for his "mercy," confident, of course, that they will get it—as in the case of the two blind men in Matthew 9:27. They cite his enemies complaining that he is "friend of the [despised] tax collectors and sinners"—as Jesus insists they complain in Luke 7:34. Can we not call such an attitude and such behavior "love"? The evangelists, however, do not use the term. Only Mark speaks of Jesus' "love" and that only once. When in 10:21 he describes the Master's reaction to the rich man's apparently sincere declaration that he had kept all the Law's commandments ever since his youth, he says, "Jesus looked at him and loved him."

The disciples and God. Faith means accepting Jesus as more than a merely ordinary man, as the man in whom God acts. Jesus notes the faith of those who request a miracle, as in the narrative of the centurion who asks for his servant's cure (Matthew 8:10). He elicits faith with the question, "Do you believe?" as in the story of the two blind men in Matthew 9:28. Or he declares that the healing comes in accord with the faith of the seeker, as in the account of the woman with hemorrhage in Matthew 9:22. This faith means recognizing and opening oneself to the power of God at work in Jesus. Full faith means accepting the God who acts and reveals himself in Jesus as Father. When, for example, his disciples fail to depend completely on the heavenly Father's concern for their food and clothing, he tells them they have little faith. Faith, then, means to accept God as Father. Father means love. Faith means to accept God as love.

If God is Father and Father means love, then we would expect the attitude towards God of a man who has by faith accepted him as Father to be a return of love. In all three Synoptic Gospels (Mark 12:29-30; Matthew 22:37-38; Luke 10:25-28) Jesus singles out Deuteronomy's command to love God with one's whole heart and life and strength as the foremost and greatest commandment in the entire Mosaic Law. Not rarely contemporary rabbis posed the problem of the relative importance of the Law's various prescriptions. When a scribe, or lawyer, puts the question to Jesus, the teacher from Nazareth refers his questioner to the one Old Testament book which used the term "love" to describe the wholehearted devotion to God that should characterize the convinced Israelite. Even more, he goes on to inform the inquirer that on this commandment and another which he links with it depends everything else in the Old Testament. But, as we shall see below, it is on this second commandment that he places the emphasis. Elsewhere in warning against selfish concern for material goods, Jesus stresses the need of complete and unlimited devotion to God. He once again calls this devotion "love." "A man cannot serve two masters," he says. "He will either hate the one and love the other, or he will be devoted to the one and despise the other. You cannot serve God and mammon" (Matthew 6:24; Luke 16:13). Two texts, both of them directing the attention more to some other point (the second commandment or the danger of avarice), are not very extensive grounds for concluding that love for God is the basic attitude God's children should have towards their heavenly Father. Perhaps Jesus (and the Synoptic evangelists) felt that faith—the faith which effectively accepts God as Father and leads a man to imitate him—was a clear enough designation for man's proper attitude to God and that therefore there was little need to speak of love for him.

Jesus demands total devotion to himself just as he demands it in his Father's regard. The reason is, of course, that men can find the Father and be devoted to him only as he reveals himself in and through Jesus. The word "love" and a term meaning "cherish" or "love tenderly" describe this devotion. In Matthew 10:37 Jesus warns, "Anyone who cherishes father or mother, . . . son or daughter more than me is not worthy of me." In Luke 7:42-47 he connects the sinful woman's show of love for himself with the forgiveness of her faults.

The Synoptic Gospels, then, quite emphatically present the Father's relationship to his Son Jesus as love. They leave us to conclude for ourselves that in sharing Jesus' relationship to the Father we share in the Father's love for him and that in accepting God by faith as Father we accept him as love. They also present Jesus as exalting love for God above all other precepts of the Old Law. But they do not insist on this overly much. There is one other area in which they do employ the term—the one in which they employ it most frequently and even more emphatically and novelly than when speaking of the Father's relation to Jesus—that is, love of neighbor.

The disciples and their fellow men. In declaring love for God the first and greatest commandment of the Old Law, Jesus links another with it as second greatest (Mark 12:28-31), like the first and forming with the first that on which the entire Old Law depends (Matthew 22:35-40) or forming with the first a single commandment whose observance assures a man of "life" (Luke 10:25-28). This commandment is the commandment of Leviticus 19:18 which we examined above: "You must love your neighbor as yourself." To declare it the second greatest commandment of the Old Law despite the rather secondary importance it has in the Old Testament is, to say the least, rather startling. It is even more startling to see what Jesus does with it.

If with all its limitations in Leviticus 19 (love for a fellow Israelite manifested more negatively—not holding a grudge or taking vengeance—than positively) Jesus declares it the second greatest commandment of the Old Law, he wants his disciples under the New Dispensation to have a love of neighbor that goes far beyond it. To the lawyer's question in Luke 10:29, "Who is my neighbor?" the Master replies with the parable of the Good Samaritan. He says in effect: you must act as a neighbor, prove yourself a neighbor, to everyone without exception even those for whom you feel a positive repulsion—since the Jews and the Samaritans had nothing to do with one another (see Sirach 50:25-26, examined above, and John 4:9).

So too in the Sermon on the Mount (Matthew 5:1-7:29 and, more briefly, Luke 6:20-49) Jesus insists that his followers may not merely follow the Old Law's command. "You have heard," he explains, "that it was said, 'You must love your neighbor'—but may hate your enemy. But I say to you," he adds, "'Love [even] your enemies.'" These enemies in the context of the sermon (see Matthew 5:1-12) include religious persecutors—enemies of God himself.

The love Jesus prescribes extends, then, to all men without exception even the very least deserving. It is an active love which prays for persecutors and (in Luke) does good to those who hate and blesses those who curse. If they show love like this, the disciples' righteousness exceeds that of the scribes and Pharisees as Jesus says it must if they are to enjoy God's reign over their lives (Matthew 5:20). Indeed, their righteousness exceeds any ever before proposed to men. It will make them like God.

Jesus says as much in the very passage we are examining (Matthew 5:45): "Love [even] your enemies . . . ," he demands, "so that you may behave as children of your Father in heaven." Then he goes on to explain how God acts in the same kindly way towards his enemies in giving the evil and the unjust sun and rain just as he gives these blessings to the good and the just. He insists that love limited to those who will return love for love will leave his disciples no better than the despised tax collectors and the gentiles, the typical sinners in the minds of his hearers. The disciples must, instead, be perfect as their heavenly Father is perfect or, as Luke has it, kindly and tender as their Father is.

The rule of thumb which he gives them (Matthew 7:12; Luke 6:31) is simple, "Do to men [all of them without exception] everything that you would want them to do to you"—not a negative rule such as we find among some of Jesus' contemporaries: "Avoid doing to others anything that you would dislike having done to you," but a positive and very extensive one: "Let it be your concern to do for all others whatever you consider good." In Matthew he adds, "This is the Law and the Prophets," declaring the sort of love he preaches the sum of Old Testament teaching (and even more than merely the sum) just as in Matthew 22:40 he declares the whole Law and the Prophets to depend on the two commandments of love of God and of neighbor.

The emphasis on love for neighbor carries through from the first of Jesus' sermons in the Gospels, the Sermon on the Mount, to the very last. If in the first of his sermons in Matthew he presents love of neighbor as the mark of God's children and the sum of their obligations, in the last two he presents it as the criterion by which they will be judged.

The parable of the Unmerciful Debtor occurs as the climax and close of the sermon in Matthew 18, the so-called Ecclesiastical Discourse concerning the relationships of Jesus' disciples with one another within the community they form. Jesus emphasizes self-forgetfulness, forgiveness, and concern for others. He concludes with our parable. Its lesson is simply this: God will refuse his forgiveness or "mercy" or "compassion" to men who have refused "mercy" to others. This application of the important Old Testament law of talion ("an eye for an eye, a tooth for a tooth . . .") to a man's treatment of his neighbor as the criterion of God's judgment of him, the only application found in the Synoptic Gospels, is suggested elsewhere. For example, Jesus warns after teaching the "Our Father," "If you forgive men their transgressions, your heavenly Father will also forgive you; if you do not forgive men, neither will your Father forgive you your transgressions" (Matthew 6:14-15). Again, among the beatitudes he includes, "Happy are those who show mercy, for mercy will be shown to them"—by God, of course (5:7). There is probably the implication that this forgiveness and mercy are forgiveness and mercy to be shown at the judgment. In the parable of the Unmerciful Debtor, however, the implication is most obvious of all. In the parable of the Last Judgment, which concludes Jesus' discourse on his coming as judge (Matthew 24-25), it becomes explicit.

In this final parable of the Matthean account of the public ministry (Matthew 25:31-46) Jesus declares quite simply that a man's care for the needs of his neighbor or neglect of them will be the criterion by which he himself will decide that man's eternity. Although the term "love" does not occur or even the term "mercy," can we fail to recognize the acts mentioned—feeding the hungry, clothing the naked, caring for the sick . . .—as acts of mercy or love? In short, the man who loves is saved; the man who does not is condemned.

In view of the emphasis on love of neighbor throughout the rest of the Gospel, it seems altogether unnecessary to imagine any sort of exaggeration—as though Jesus meant to underscore the importance of love for neighbor by speaking *as if* he would judge us on it alone though in fact he will not. If love of neighbor is really the proof or mark of God's children, making a man like God, and if "eternal life" or God's "kingdom" is meant for those who share in Jesus' filial relationship to the Father, it is quite simply to those who love and to them alone that Jesus can say, "Come, you blessed of my Father, take possession of the kingdom prepared for you . . ." (25:34).

But this final parable has yet another ray of light to shed on the love for fellow men that Jesus preaches. He does not in fact tell the saved that he rewards them because their kind deeds have proved them children of the Father. He says, "*I* was hungry and you gave *me* to eat. . . . As long as you did it to one of these least of my brothers, you did it to *me*." And to the condemned he complains, "I was hungry and you did not give me to eat. . . . As long as you did not do it to one of these least ones, you did not do it to me." The object of their care or neglect has not been just a lowly human being but Jesus himself.

Earlier Gospel sayings suggest this identity. For example, Jesus points out that a mere cup of cold water given a man as a disciple of his will not go unrewarded (Mark 9:41; Matthew 10:42). Even more clearly, he declares that welcome given the least child in his name is really welcome given him (Mark 9:37; Luke 9:48; Matthew 18:5), just as welcome offered him is welcome given the one who sent him (Mark and Luke, *ibid.*). But in the parable of the Last Judgment the just and the sinners are not even aware that Jesus has been the object of their care or neglect. They ask, "When did we see you hungry . . . ?" Whether he realizes it or not, the object of a man's love or neglect for his neighbor is Jesus, and therefore such love or neglect calls for the reward of everlasting life in the kingdom his Father has prepared or rejection into the everlasting fire prepared for the devil and his angels, those powers that stand opposed to God.

In short, then, Jesus sets love of neighbor—and a love of neighbor far beyond anything known before him—right at the center of his conception of the proper divine-human relationship. If he cites Leviticus 19:18 as the second greatest commandment of the Old Law, he does not merely hand it on to his disciples unchanged. The love he demands must go out sincerely and effectively to every man, even the least deserving. It prays, blesses, does good, forgives, gives food, drink, clothing, shelter, and other care; forgetful of self, it does all that it judges real good. If man's proper relation to God is a matter of sharing in Jesus' sonship, the manifest mark of that sonship is this love that reflects God's own. But also the neighbor who is object of the love exhibited turns out to be one with Jesus. Thus the love of neighbor that Jesus demands starts from God, reflecting his and Jesus' own, and ends in God, being love for Jesus himself.

Summary. Jesus is God's beloved Son: his only Son and the Son for whom he has a unique love. But God is Father to Jesus' disciples too. Hence, we conclude that they too are the objects of the love that the Father has for his only Son. Jesus' own behavior shows what God's love is like: he goes about doing good and delivering men from the power of the devil.

The disciples accept God as Father by their faith, and this implies loving him too. It also implies imitating him. This they do by fulfilling the commandment to love their neighbor—the second greatest commandment of the Old Law, like the great commandment (to love God), and even forming only one commandment with it. But Jesus insists that the disciples' love for neighbor must surpass Old Testament love of neighbor; it must resemble their heavenly Father's love in extending to all men, even persecutors, and in effectively seeking the good of others. Their fulfillment of this commandment is the criterion by which Jesus will judge them.

The disciples' love for their neighbor is love for Jesus himself (and therefore for God) since he is one with the neighbor they love.

LOVE IN THE PAULINE EPISTLES

The New Testament letters ascribed to Saint Paul were written for the most part before the Synoptic Gospels. The bulk of the material in the first three Gospels, however, goes back in oral form to the time of Jesus himself. The evangelists interpreted, but especially recorded and edited, these sacred and official traditions of the first-century Church about the work and teachings of Jesus. The writers of the epistles, on the other hand, largely offered their own exhortations to a good Christian life and their own explanations of the Christian message. Though they worked with the teachings and facts about Jesus' life and saving work as tradition preserved them, they reflected upon them, theologized about them, and made specific applications of them to the needs of this or that community or individual. Hence, they show a later and more developed appreciation of the Christian message than the Synoptic Gospels do. This is true especially of the Pauline epistles.

The Father and the Son. For Paul, of course, as for the Synoptics, God is Father, above all, of Jesus—"the God and Father of our Lord Jesus Christ," as he so often calls him. For Paul, as for the evangelists, to say "father" is to say "love." If the first three Gospels in three very important texts designate Jesus as God's "beloved Son," the Pauline epistles do so in two. In Colossians 1:13 Paul describes God's saving work as his delivering us "from the power of the darkness and [bringing] us into the kingdom of the Son of his love, in whom we have redemption." The expression "Son of his love" sounds just as unusual in the Greek language in which Paul wrote as it does in English, but it is quite correct in his native Aramaic and means "his beloved son." Ephesians, an epistle patterned on Colossians and probably composed for a wider reading public, describes God's same saving work in 1:5-6 as his making us his sons through Jesus Christ, a favor or "grace he has shown us in the beloved [Jesus], in whom we have redemption." The adjective "beloved" which occurs in the Gospels emphasizes the uniqueness of Jesus' sonship (it is the usual Old Testament expression for "*only* son") as much as it does the Father's paternal affection for him. The Pauline texts use not this adjective but the noun "love" (Colossians) and the participle of the verb "to love" (Ephesians), thus emphasizing the fatherly affection of God for his Son even more than the unique nature of Jesus' relationship to him.

In both these passages, interestingly, the writer lays his emphasis less on the relationship of Jesus and the Father than on the relationship we enjoy with the Father in and through Christ. In Colossians

Paul explains that God has delivered us from darkness and brought us into the kingdom of his Son, made us one with him in the Church, so as to have us holy, spotless, and blameless in his sight (1:12-23). The Ephesians text forms part of a hymn to God's saving work in Christ: in him he chose us to be holy and spotless (our election); through him he predestined us for sonship (our predestination); in him we have redemption; in him he intends to effect the restoration of all things (1:3-14). The special relationship Christ has to the Father serves to explain the special relationship to him which we enjoy because of our union with Christ.

The Father and believing Christians. If Jesus is the beloved Son, we would expect Paul to treat Christians as God's beloved. He does this quite frequently. In his earliest epistles, the two he wrote to the persecuted Christian community at Thessalonica, he designates his Christian addressees as his "brothers loved by God" (1 Thessalonians 1:4) or "by the Lord" (2 Thessalonians 2:13). He is surely thinking of the expression "Yahweh's beloved" which the Old Testament used to designate Israel as Yahweh's chosen people. His comparison of the Thessalonian church's situation to that of the persecuted communities in Judea (1 Thessalonians 2:14-16) makes one wonder whether he is not already thinking of the conviction he expresses in later letters (for example, Romans 9-11) that the Jews (and gentiles) who accepted Jesus as the Christ formed the true Israel while the unbelieving are simply fallen-aways. If he is, then he quite rightly designates them "God's beloved" as the Old Testament designated Israel. But Paul is not merely employing a stereotype. If Christians are God's beloved, it is because of what God has done for them in Christ. This effective manifestation of his immense and paternal good will which freely gives us "unending consolation and a solid hope" proves him "God our Father who loved us" (2 Thessalonians 2:16).

The Roman Christians too are for Paul "God's beloved" (Romans 1:7). Once again the Old Testament use of the expression to designate Israel as God's chosen ones seems to be in his mind: the Christians of Rome are God's "beloved" because in Christ they have been called, that is, chosen, to be holy to him (1:6). But here again Paul is not simply employing a cliché; the proof lies in his description in chapters 5 and 8 of what God has done for us in Christ as an expression of divine love.

The great manifestation of divine love consists in Christ's having died for us when we were sinners (5:8). God's having had his very Son die for sinners, his enemies, can hardly be fittingly described by any other term than "love"—a wholly undeserved yet incredibly great show of affection that effectively reconciled us with him. So mighty and persistent is this divine affection that Paul can declare all creatures utterly incapable of frustrating or undoing it. It turns the very attempts made against its designs into occasions for furthering them (8:35-39):

"Who can separate us from the love of Christ? Tribulation or distress or persecution or hunger or nakedness or peril or the sword? . . . Rather, in [*or* by means of] these things we are more than victorious because of him who loved us. For I am sure that neither death nor life, nor angels whether principalities or powers, neither things present nor things future, neither height nor depth, nor any other creature can separate us from the love of God [*or* the love which God has shown us] in Christ Jesus our Lord."

Christ's death for us sinners is, then, the great manifestation of divine love, but with that death we must include everything that follows upon it: Christ's resurrection, which according to 6:4-11 gave us our new life (for "he was handed over for our transgressions and rose for our justification"—4:25), and the outpouring of the divine Spirit, whose guiding presence in our hearts according to 8:11-17 makes us God's sons in Christ and assures us of final resurrection (our "hope does not disappoint because God's love has been poured out into our hearts by the holy Spirit that has been given us"—5:5). All that Christ has done, then—the entire Christ-event—is a manifestation of divine love. Needless to say, it is also an expression of Christ's own love. Indeed, it is this love that Christ has shown which effectively manifests the love that God has.

Romans is not the only Pauline epistle which so clearly presents the Christ-event in terms of love. Ephesians, for example, does the same. What God did in Christ to save sinners may be called an act of "mercy" (the term Paul usually uses to underscore the misery of those whom God helps). It may also be called an act of "grace," that is, favor (the term the Pauline writings employ to emphasize the gratuitous character of God's help). But, above all, it must be called an act of love. After a description of the moral misery of gentile and Jew before Christ (2:1-3) comes the declaration: "Now God, since he is rich in mercy, because of his great love with which he loved us, even though we were dead in our transgressions, gave us life with and in Christ (by grace you have been saved); he both raised us and seated us in the heavens with and in Christ Jesus so that he might manifest to the coming ages the superabundant riches of his grace in the kindness [he showed us] in Christ Jesus" (Ephesians 2:4-7).

The epistle to Titus, dating from very late in the Apostle's life and even thought by some to have been composed by a disciple after his death, contains the same teaching. Chapter 2 (verses 11-14) describes Christ's handing of himself over on our behalf to free us from wickedness and to make us a people of God's own possession as an epiphany to all men of the saving favor, or grace, of God and a preparation for the final glorious epiphany of the divine Savior. Then after a digression urging Titus to press home their duties to his community, the thought of our own deliverance from sin by Christ returns, but this time as the epiphany of divine love (3:4-7): "When the kindness and tender affection for men of God our savior made its appearance [*or* epiphany], it was not because of any righteous works that we had done but in accord with his own mercy that he saved us. He did it through the bath of regeneration and renewal in the holy Spirit. This Spirit he poured out upon us abundantly through Jesus Christ our Savior so that made righteous by his grace we might in accord with our hope come into our inheritance of eternal life." The word "love" (*agápē*) does not occur. Instead, we find God's "tender affection for men" (*philanthrōpía*). Possibly the latter word occurs because God is said, at least in 2:11, to have manifested his divine favor to *all* men and the Pauline epistles seem to reserve the term "love" for the divine beneficence that effectively achieves its purpose of saving men. We shall return to this phenomenon later when we treat the Johannine writings. In any case, it is clear that the Pauline writings from first to last look upon Christians as the objects and beneficiaries of God's *love*—a love visibly and tangibly manifested in the love Christ showed for miserable and totally undeserving sinners by dying, rising, and sending the Spirit to give us a share in his glory.

Christians and God. The Father loves his Son. The Father loves us in him; because of our union with him we are objects of the same paternal love of God. That love has become manifest in what Christ did for us, active in him to make us its objects. We must respond to or accept the divine initiative. Our response is faith. The object of that faith is the "truth" (2 Thessalonians 2:13) or the "gospel," that is, the good news (Philippians 1:27). But the content of this good news is Christ—more precisely, the crucified and risen Christ (1 Thessalonians 4:14; Romans 1:2-4; 2 Timothy 2:8). More precisely still, it is God who acts in and through Christ, raising him from the dead and giving life through and in him (Galatians 2-3; Romans 3-4). Faith means accepting God as the savior he shows himself to be in Christ. It means acceptance, submission, surrender, saying yes to him, for we believe "in"—more accurately, "upon" or "into"—him. By faith we are "justified," that is, become righteous, have life, become God's sons in Christ (*ibid.*). Since the divine self-revelation which we accept by faith is the revelation of divine love, faith means accepting God as love. Paul says as much in Galatians 2:20, where after describing God's saving act in Christ, he adds, "It is no longer I that live: Christ lives in me; the life that I continue to live in the flesh [that is, in my present weak human condition] I live in my faith in the Son of God who loved me and handed himself over on my behalf."

We might have expected Paul to speak of love for God as our response to his love—as Deuteronomy speaks of love (meaning wholehearted devotion) as Israel's expected response to the gratuitous divine love (meaning God's election-love). After all, submission to the revelation he makes or the initiative he takes in Christ is an absolute and total surrender or devotion of oneself to him. The epistles occasionally speak of those who love God (Romans 8:28; 1 Corinthians 2:9) or our Lord Jesus Christ (Ephesians 6:24) or his coming (2 Timothy 4:8). The texts are few and look suspiciously like the Old Testament stereotype which might be rendered more accurately, as we saw when speaking of the Old Testament, "God's friends." The term "faith" brings out the distinctiveness of the Christian response to God much more clearly than "love" would. But, of course, "love" (meaning total devotion) is just as correct, if not so comprehensive, a description.

The Christian and others. On the other hand, love is the best term to describe the Christian's relation to his fellows. With faith in God or Christ, love for others occurs quite regularly in Paul as a characteristic mark of the Christian. Hope or endurance frequently turns the pair into a trio. From the earliest epistles (1 Thessalonians 1:3; 2 Thessalonians 1:3) to the latest (1-2 Timothy and Titus, which link faith and love eight times) the Christian appears as the man who has believed in Christ and loves his fellows.

The two are not simply unrelated marks. The Christian's love for men follows upon and flows from his faith in Christ. By faith he surrenders to a God who thereupon becomes his Father, a God who saves him by making him his son (see Galatians 3:26-27), giving him a share in his life. But the Christian revelation is that God is a loving God and it is precisely to sharing the life of a God who is all-loving that a man commits himself by Christian faith. To love, therefore, is the great task of the believer.

Paul says this explicitly in Galatians 5:6. "In Christ Jesus [that is, for the Christian] neither circumcision nor its absence has any value but only faith that expresses itself through love"—faith, that surrender to sharing the life of the God who reveals himself in Christ, a surrender which expresses itself in the life of love that the believer leads. Or a bit differently in the same epistle he argues that we who have received the divine Spirit through faith (3:2-14), the Spirit who makes us sons in Christ (4:6), must follow the impulse of the Spirit allowing him to direct our behavior (5:16), and what the Spirit impels us to is love (5:22).

Even more explicitly he points out that the Christian's love of others imitates Christ's own love. Perhaps we should understand 1 Thessalonians 4:9 in this way; there he tells the Thessalonians that he need not write them about fraternal affection since they have learned from God to love one another. Most unambiguously Ephesians 4:32-5:2 exhorts, "To each other be kind, compassionate, forgiving one another as God has forgiven you in Christ. Be imitators of God, therefore, as his beloved children, and walk in love as Christ himself loved you and handed himself over on our behalf . . ." (see also 5:25).

Nature and characteristics of this love. Paul describes this love of which he speaks as a love that goes out to all men. After all, the revelation God makes of himself in Christ is meant to be accepted by all men; it is an offer of divine love to all. If the Christian must imitate his divine Father's love, he too must love all. As Jesus does in the Synoptic Gospels, Paul too uses the command of Leviticus 19:18 about love of neighbor but reinterprets it to make it apply to much more than the Old Testament envisioned. In Romans 13:8-10, for example, he presents fulfilling the Old Testament command as the fulfillment of all precepts—Mosaic and, it would seem, all others besides. In doing this, he certainly understands the neighbor—whom he calls "the other," that is, "others" in general—as more than simply one's fellows (that is, fellow Christians). It is immediately after insisting on the payment of tribute, taxes, respect, and honor due pagan government authorities

(13:1-7) that he allows the Christian to have only one debt permanently outstanding—the debt of loving others. Certainly it is not owed only to fellow Christians.

However, just as in speaking of God's goodness he tends to reserve the designation "love" for the divine beneficence that will effectively succeed in doing the good it intends, so in speaking of the Christian's beneficence he prefers to reserve the term "love" for the beneficence which goes out to those who effectively accept it—fellow Christians. The beneficence that goes out to those who are less likely to return it is "doing good." When describing the love which along with faith characterizes the Christian, he usually designates it as love "for one another," rarely adding as he does in 1 Thessalonians 3:12, "and for all." But in Galatians 6:10 he recommends that we "do good to all," adding however even here (where the term "love" does not occur) "but especially to those who are of the household of the faith."

This love is not only the great task of the believer; it exhausts his obligations. As we have already seen, Paul declares it the only thing of value for the Christian (Galatians 5:6, examined above, page 53). As we have also seen, it is the only debt Paul wants the Christian to have outstanding (Romans 13:8, examined just above). It is also the Christian's full substitute for all the prescriptions the Mosaic Law imposed on Judaism. In writing to the Christians of

Galatia, who were enamoured of the Jewish Law and in danger of effectively abandoning Christianity to become Jews, he declares Leviticus 19:18 as a complete summary of the Old Law (Galatians 5:14): to fulfill it is to do everything. He urges them, therefore, to substitute for servitude to the detailed prescriptions of the Law's ceremonial practices the service of one another in love (5:13). But the love of which he is thinking—as we have seen in treating his use of this Old Testament text in writing to the Romans—is a love that extends far beyond the limits of Leviticus 19 (page 54).

To live by this love is to do all the Christian need do. Paul writes to the Corinthian community that any gift or ability the Christian may have, even the gift of speaking in foreign tongues, the possession of profound knowledge, the power to work miracles or to accomplish the most heroic feats, is worthless without love (1 Corinthians 13:1-3). Indeed, all of them will eventually disappear, but love lasts forever (13:8-12). Love alone assures that the Christian will use these gifts for the purpose for which God intends them: the upbuilding of the community (12:7 and 14:5). Even without them love accomplishes all the Christian need do. For love is patient and kind. It is without envy or fanfare, without insolence or shamelessness, without self-interest or anger. It is unmindful of wrongs and ready to rejoice with right, able to bear up under and endure, to believe in and hope for all situations and persons and things (13:4-7).

The pagan philosophers set man's perfection in the acquisition of various virtues. When he habitually employed each of his powers directly on its proper object, then he was perfect. This meant, for example, using food and drink with temperance and sobriety, facing difficulties with courage, treating other persons with justice. Habitual misuse of any such object constituted a vice for these thinkers—intemperance, drunkenness, pusillanimity, injustice, and so on. For Paul, the Christian cannot be intemperate, a drunkard, a coward, unjust . . .—not because these things are vices or the lack of some desirable acquired perfection. For him the Christian must show self-control, courage, fairness, and the like, because these are expressions of love and their opposites are expressions of the selfishness that excludes love. He can say quite simply, "Let all that you do be done in love" (1 Corinthians 16:14). If the Christian has by faith become a son of God, then his great—in fact, his total—task is to live his heavenly Father's life of love.

We have come to appreciate God's love in the love Christ showed for us. In accepting him by faith, we commit ourselves to imitating or sharing in his love. In a very real sense it is Christ or God who loves in us when we love because it is no longer ourselves that live but the Son of God who loved us and delivered himself up on our behalf who lives in us. But our Christian love is not only a sharing in Christ's love; it is not only Christ loving in us. It is also Christ whom we love. To paraphrase Saint Augustine's description of Christian preaching as Christ preaching Christ, Christian love is Christ loving Christ.

On the road to Damascus Christ revealed to Saul that he was really identified with Christians: "Saul, Saul, why are you persecuting me? . . . I am Jesus whom you are persecuting" (Acts 9:4-5). In this experience Paul received his basic grasp of the meaning of the Church. Throughout his epistles he avoids the term "Christians"; he speaks rather of those who are "in Christ," Christ's "body" (that is, one physical reality with him into whom baptism has inserted them and on whom they feed in the Eucharist). He denounces sins committed against Christians—against the community (1 Corinthians 3:16-17), against a brother who believes (Romans 14:15; 1 Corinthians 8:11-12), or even committed by a Christian against his own person (1 Corinthians 6:15; 2 Corinthians 6:14ff)—as sins committed against Christ, profaning or destroying those who are one with him. Christians are Christ. To do good to them, love them, is to love Christ himself. And Christ, of course, is God. Hence Paul can describe concern about a brother's weak conscience as love not simply for a fellow Christian, nor simply for Christ, but for God (1 Corinthians 8:3).

If charity is the Christian's whole life, a sharing in Christ's and God's own love, and love for Christ and God, it is by its very nature the great cohesive force that holds the Christian community together, building up the Church, welding it ever more effectively into the body of Christ. The plea in Ephesians 4:17-5:2, climaxing in the injunction that Christians as God's well-loved children imitate him by mirroring in their own behavior the love Christ showed, follows a detailed description of the Church as the community of love (4:1-16)—a picture that might well recall the ideal community sketched in Acts 2:42-47 and 4:32-35. Through their common calling by their one Father Christians form one body, have one Spirit, recognize one Lord, profess one faith in him, have all received the same baptism (or immersion) into him. Whatever differences distinguish them from one another are only so many divinely bestowed gifts meant to serve for the upbuilding of the community: the very differences are meant to make those who have them more effectively one in and with Christ. But what their unity consists in and what assures the successful achievement of the purpose for which God has bestowed on them the various gifts is love: the body builds itself up in love. Although there is no mention of the Eucharist here, it seems natural to recall that according to 1 Corinthians it is the Eucharist, which commemorates Christ's great act of love, his death (11:26), that causes the unity of the Church (10:16-17).

Summary. We may sketch the general outline of Saint Paul's conception of Christianity in terms of love with a few brief strokes. The "God and Father of our Lord Jesus Christ" loves his Son. He loves us in him. What God has done for us in Christ—in particular, his passion and resurrection and the sending of the Spirit—is a revelation of the immense divine love. In experiencing Christ's love for us we come to some appreciation of the Father's. Our response to the divine initiative is faith—a "yes," a submission, a surrender to the designs of divine love on our lives. But we are not only those who have believed in Christ or in God; we are also those who love him. To submit to God's design to make us his sons, one with his Son, means to submit to living God's own life, and this means "walking in love," that is, living a life of love. Our love, like God's and Christ's, must go out to all and must do so always. In going out to others, it is actually going out to Christ himself—is love for Christ and God—because those others are one with him. To love is our one great Christian task. Faith and the love that follows upon it alone have value in our life. Without love nothing in our life has worth. Love satisfies all obligations, excludes the sin that would block God's work in our life, assures the good use of all divine gifts we may have. It is the vitality and the cohesive force that binds the Church together and makes it grow.

LOVE IN THE JOHANNINE WRITINGS

The fourth Gospel and the three epistles of Saint John are among the latest of the New Testament writings. They evidence a long meditation of the gospel message on the part of their author—a meditation engaged in against the background of the great threat to Christianity in late first-century Asia Minor: denial that God had really become man in Christ. The Gospel presents the good news of Christ in such a way as to show its readers (who had never known him in the flesh) that they still hear his words in the preaching of the Church and still come into contact with him in her sacraments—the historical Jesus of Nazareth, who was the awaited Messiah and, even more, the Son of God become man, the revelation of the Father to men. It insists that the good things Judaism awaited have already come with Christ, even if there is still more to come, and that we enjoy them in the Church. The epistles, especially the first and the second, suppose this outlook on Christianity.

For John, Jesus is God's Word made flesh, that is, his (final and full) self-expression or self-communication in human form. All that Jesus says and all that he does, especially his passion and resurrection, show what he is and, since he is God's self-revelation, what God is. What he reveals about God is that God is Father (because he is Son) or rather that God is our Father if we accept his self-communication in Jesus by faith. All of this is succinctly summarized in a few verses of the Gospel's prologue (John 1:1-18). Practically the only point that we need add to the prologue's assertions to have a complete outline of John's thought is the conviction which the rest of the Gospel shows that the great and definitive act of Jesus which made his (and the Father's) identity undeniably clear, his "glorification," was his passion and resurrection.

Father and Son. The identity of Jesus as Son in an altogether unique sense appears in the unique relationship he has with God. He does what he sees the Father doing; he can do nothing else (John 5). The Father shows him all that he does (5:20) and has put everything in his hand (3:35). But what inspires the Father's doing this is his love for the Son. "The Father loves the Son and has put all things in his hand" (3:35); "the Father cherishes the Son and shows him all that he himself does" (5:20). At the same time, the Father loves him because he corresponds so fully to the Father's initiative: "The Father loves me," Jesus says, "because I lay down my life so that I may take it up again. . . . This commandment I have received from my Father" (10:17-18). Or, to express the same idea a bit differently, by his docility to the Father's lead he maintains himself in the Fathers love: ". . . the Father has loved me . . . ," he tells his disciples. "I have kept my Father's commands," he goes on, "and [thereby] remain in his love" (15:9-10).

The Father's love, therefore, gives Jesus the unique role he has of revealing the Father to men; by his docility to the Father's lead he keeps himself in the Father's love. But the fulfillment of that unique role means, above all, passion and resurrection. The work to which docility to the Father's lead will bring him consists especially in laying down his life in order to take it up again. And this act of obedience to the divine command Jesus presents as an expression of his own love for the Father: he concludes his discourse in chapter 14 with the reason why he goes out of the supper room to accost the prince of the world: "that the world may know that I love the Father and do just as the Father has commanded me" (14:31).

Father, Son, and ourselves. The Father loves the Son. The Son maintains himself in the Father's love by loving the Father with a love that expresses itself in obedience to the Father's command. The Father's command is that Jesus love us and so reveal the Father's love for us—for the fourth Gospel and the first Johannine epistle quite emphatically present the passion-resurrection as a manifestation of love.

The epistle perhaps most simply of all: "This is how we have come to know love: he [Christ] has laid down his life on our behalf" (3:16).

The love manifested is, first, Jesus' own love. When the evangelist begins his passion account with the Supper narrative in chapter 13, he solemnly underscores that Jesus' "hour had come to pass from this world to the Father," and he declares this passage Jesus' great act of love for his own: "having loved his own who were in the world, he loved them to the end"—not simply the end of his life but to the very limits of possible demonstrations of love (13:1). During the Supper discourses Jesus himself declares, "No one has greater love than to lay down his life for those whom he cherishes; you are those whom I cherish" (15:13-14).

The passion-resurrection is just as emphatically a manisfestation of the Father's love. In fact, the evangelist's public ministry account practically opens on this note. At the end of Jesus' conversation with Nicodemus in John 3 we find a solemn declaration: "God so loved the world as to give his only-begotten Son so that everyone who believes in him might not be lost but might enjoy possession of life everlasting" (3:16). The first epistle uses almost the very same words. "The love of God has become manifest among us in that God has sent his only-begotten Son into the world that we might enjoy life through him" (4:9). The author explains, "The love lies in this:

we had not loved God, but he loved us and sent his Son as expiation for our sins" (4:10). This text echoes Romans 5:8, examined above (page 47): "God commends his love to us in that Christ died on our behalf while we were still sinners." We may conclude that in Christ's great act of love we have come to know the love of the Father, whom he reveals.

Our response to the initiative God's love takes, for John as for Paul, is faith. (It may be well to note that already John 3:16, the fourth Gospel's very first mention of love, lays this faith down as condition for the achievement of the saving designs of divine love: "God so loved the world as to give . . . that *everyone who believes* might not be lost. . . .") Faith is what God demands of man (6:29). It is the indispensable condition for having life and escaping judgment (5:24), for avoiding death (8:24), and for receiving the divine Spirit (7:38-39). It is the reaction of a man to all Jesus says and does (10:37-38). As many of the above-cited texts and many others show, faith means accepting Jesus for what he really is: "the Christ, the Son of God come into the world" (11:26-27; see 20:31). It means, therefore, coming to "know," that is, recognize and experience, God in him (10:38; 14:9-11). Since the full revelation of Jesus' identity lies in that final great manifestation of his glory which consists in his passion-resurrection and which is called quite simply his "glorification" (see 12:27-28 and 17:1-2), full acceptance of him for what he is—full faith—is not possible until then (see, for example, 2:22; 3:14-15; 8:28). Now if the passion-resurrection is a great act of love, then acceptance of this final full manifestation of God is the acceptance of divine love or the acceptance of God as love. This is exactly what the first Johannine epistle says (4:14-16): ". . . the Father has sent the Son as savior of the world. . . . We have come to know and believe the love which God has for us."

The Pauline writings mention love for God rather rarely. The Johannine writings also do so rarely. The only sure text occurs in 1 John 4:20-5:2—a passage to which we shall return later. The ambiguous expression "love of God" or "love of the Father," which can mean either love for God or God's own love, occurs with some frequency. We shall return to it later, too. John avoids the Old Testament stereotype "those who love God." If he speaks of love for God at all, it is in the context of love for others or for Christ. Not love but faith, that is, the acceptance of the God whom Christ reveals as love, is the distinctively Christian relationship to God.

Love for Christ occurs more often in the Johannine writings. After having appealed for faith throughout the whole of his public ministry, Jesus at the Supper table with those who are presumably committed to making the surrender of faith begins to speak of love. The love he asks them to show is love for himself, a love expressed in observance of his commands just as the love for God which Deuteronomy commends shows itself in keeping his commands (14:15-24). But it is a warm personal love too which rejoices in Jesus' victory (14:28). Just as Jesus himself shows his love for the Father by keeping the Father's commands (14:31) and by that same obedience maintains himself in the Father's love (15:10), so his disciples by their obedience to his commands not only show love for him but maintain themselves in his love: "As the Father has loved me," he tells them, "I too have loved you. Remain in my love. If you keep my commandments, you will remain in my love as I have kept my Father's commandments and remain in his love" (15:9-10). We may go a step further. Since Jesus' love is a manifestation of the Father's love, by loving Jesus and maintaining themselves in Jesus' love the disciples maintain themselves in the Father's love: "The Father," Jesus tells them, "cherishes you because you have cherished me and have believed that I came out from God" (16:27).

If we ask what these commandments are which we must obey to show our love, the answer is quite simple: there is only one—that we love one another.

Fraternal or mutual relations. The commandment to love our fellows holds as central a place in John as it does in the Synoptic Gospels and the Pauline epistles. We might say it holds an even more central place. The first three Gospels and Paul speak of other principles of conduct besides love—poverty, celibacy, humility, and the like (though, of course, they are all reducible to love as in 1 Corinthians 13). The Johannine Gospel and epistles do not even mention any other principles.

After appealing for faith in himself throughout his public ministry, Jesus in his Supper discourses introduces an appeal for love of neighbor, presenting this appeal in the form of the one commandment he gives. In 13:34, at the very start of the discourses, he announces: "A new commandment I give you: that you love one another." He even adds, "This is how all men will know that you are my disciples: by your love for one another" (13:35). In 15:12, just after insisting that it is obedience to his commands that will keep them in his love, he explains: "This is my commandment: that you love one another . . ." (see 15:17).

The Johannine epistles insist on no other command but the commandment of fraternal love. It is an old commandment for Christians in that it goes back to the beginnings of Christianity; it is a new commandment too in that it was not given before Christ (1 John 2:7-8; 2 John 5). It is the message we have heard from the beginning of our call to Christianity (1 John 3:11). "This is his commandment—" John writes in 3:23, "that we believe in the name of his son Jesus Christ and that we love one another. . . ." This translation does not do justice to the nuances expressed in the original Greek. A difference of tense in the verbs "believe" and "love" makes clear that the faith is something given once and for all while the love is something to be given continually. We might perhaps more accurately translate, "This is his commandment—that we who have believed in his Son Jesus Christ go on loving one another." The text is reminiscent of Paul's exclamation in Galatians 5:6: "In Christ Jesus neither circumcision nor its absence has any value but only faith which expresses itself through love."

Love, then, is the one precept incumbent on Christians. For the believer, to fulfill it is to do everything. The reason is just as clear in John as in the Synoptics and in Paul but is expressed somewhat differently. By faith we accept Jesus as God's self-revelation. "Self-communication" might be a better word. He reveals, or communicates, God by his words and works—above all, by his passion-resurrection. To accept the divine self-communication by faith will necessarily change our lives: we will have to start living like Christ—which means like God. Jesus' precept governing our conduct, then, can only be to imitate his own conduct, to be in our behavior what he shows himself to be by his. It is noteworthy that in John 14 Jesus' "words," which, interchangeably with his works (14:10), reveal his identity so that the disciples can accept him by faith (14:11), are also interchangeable with his "commandments" (compare 14:15-21 and 14:23-24). His preceptive word is that we be what his revelatory word shows him and the Father to be. By faith we accept God's communication of himself as love, and by love of one another we live by the divine self-communication we have received.

In giving his new commandment, Jesus does not prescribe merely that we love one another. He insists that we love one another as he has loved us, and he refers explicitly to that great manifestation of his love (and of God as love), his passion. In 13:34, he gives the "new commandment" after having washed the disciples' feet (an act which symbolized the fast-approaching passion, that act of self-humiliation which he had to perform on their behalf if they were to enjoy union with him—13:8), and the commandment is "that you love one another just as I have loved you." In 15:12 it is the commandment "that you love one another as I have loved you"; and he adds immediately: "No one has greater love than to lay down his life for those whom he cherishes; you are those whom I cherish" (15:13-14).

It is understandable now how Jesus could declare fraternal love the distinguishing mark of his disciples (John 13:35). It is understandable too that John in his first epistle should indicate fraternal love as the proof of our joyful "community" of "life" with God (see 1 John 1-3). We must walk in the light (because God is light) to have community with him (1:5-7).

We must keep his commands or his word in order to know him (2:3-5). We must walk as he (Christ) walked if we are to remain in him (2:6). But to be in the light, to keep his commandment, and to walk as he did means to love our brothers (2:7-11). Fraternal love is, therefore, the proof and manifestation of the life within us: "We know that we have passed over from death to life because we love our brothers" (3:14).

Most explicitly, in chapter 4 of the first epistle, John explains quite simply that God is love and that therefore anyone who by faith has become a child of God must love. "Beloved," he writes, "let us love on another, for love is from God, and everyone who loves has been born of God [that is, is God's child] and knows God [in the Hebrew sense of experiencing him]. A man who does not love has not known God, for God is love." He continues with the idea we have already seen: Christ has come to reveal God's love. "This is how the manifestation of God's love was made among us: God sent his only-begotten Son into the world that we might enjoy life through him. The love lies in this: we did not love God [—we were sinners], but he loved us and sent his Son as expiation for our sins" (verses 9-10). He passes to the practical conclusion that we who have accepted sharing the life of such a God must therefore love: "Beloved, if God has so loved us, we too must love one another. No one has ever seen

God; if we love one another, God remains in us, and his love has reached its fullness in us" (verses 11-12). After insisting that by our faith in the crucified-risen Christ we have believed in God as love ("we have believed the love which God has for us"), he sums up: "God is love, and the man who remains in love remains in God and God remains in him" (verse 16).

This last text places us in a position to consider the ambiguous phrase mentioned earlier: "the love of God." This love is described in 1 John 4:12 as reaching its perfection. Surely there it is God's own love within us with which we are loving. May this not be its meaning when it occurs elsewhere?

In John 5:42, when Jesus accuses the unbelieving Jews of not having the "love of God within them" (just as in 5:38 they do not have his "word" in them), does he mean they do not believe in him because they do not love God (or believe his word), or may he perhaps mean they cannot accept him and even want to do away with him (5:18) because they do not have God's own love within them, a love that shows itself in his honoring Jesus and wanting all men to honor him too (5:20-23)? Note how he insists in 8:42, "If God were your Father, you would love me," just after having emphasized that sonship means imitation (8:39).

Surely in the first epistle, where he speaks of the love of God in man, he is thinking of God's own love: when, for example, in 2:5 he says that "love of God has reached its fullness" in the man who keeps his commandment of fraternal love, he adds that anyone who claims union with God must "walk as he himself walked" (2:6). When in 3:17 he asks how the love of God can remain in the person who refuses to show love, he does so immediately after explaining, "This is how we have come to know love: he [Christ] laid down his life on our behalf; we too [therefore] must lay down our lives on behalf of the brothers" (3:16).

Perhaps the passage which throws most light on the meaning of the expression is 1 John 3. John begins, "See what great love the Father has *given* us that we should be called God's children and actually be such" (verse 1). He goes on to point out our (consequent) sharing of his rejection by the world. He notes the even greater assimilation to him we await at his final appearance (verse 2). He insists on our need to become more and more like him (verse 3). He explains that this means rejection of sin, which Christ came to destroy (verses 4-6). In short, he who sins is the devil's child not God's; he who acts righteously is God's child with God's "seed" within him (verses 7-9). But the righteous behavior of God's children is love, and the sinful behavior of the devil's children is the lack of love, or hatred (verses 10-11). In making us his children, therefore, God has not "given" us love merely in the sense of having loved us; he has given us his own love to have it within ourselves and to love our brothers with it.

On the other hand, John does speak of love for God. Just as for Paul (and for the Synoptics too) love for those who are one with Christ is love for Christ and ultimately God (see 1 Corinthians 8:3), so for John fraternal love is love for Christ and ultimately for God. After having declared that "God is love" and that therefore we, God's children, must love ("Let us love because he has first loved us," 1 John 4:19), he explains this (fraternal) love as really being love for God. He first affirms the unity of love for God and fraternal love. "If anyone says, 'I love God,' and hates his brother, he is a liar. He who does not love the brother whom he sees cannot love the God whom he does not see" (verse 20). He explains (5:1): "Everyone who believes that Jesus is the Christ has been begotten of God, and everyone who loves the one who begets loves the one begotten of him," that is, other believers (or possibly Jesus, with whom they are one). "This," he says (5:2-3), "is how we know we love God's children—when we love God and keep his commandments (for the love of God means keeping his commandments), and his commandments are not hard"—simply to love one another (see 3:23).

The love which we have been examining has appeared regularly as love of "one another" or of "the brothers." The Johannine writings do not contain the

Leviticus text on love of neighbor which the Synoptics and Paul cite and then reinterpret in a more universal sense. In John Jesus' command to love one another as he has loved us replaces it. The clause "as I have loved you" certainly brings out quite clearly an essential trait of Christian love of neighbor: what makes it really Christian is that it mirrors or shares in Christ's love. But the "one another" and "the brothers," the expressions that replace the "neighbor," seem to restrict it once more to the narrow limits of the Leviticus precept—to one's fellows only.

We must admit quite frankly that the Johannine writings never speak of love of enemies or even of all men. But we must also recall that Paul does so rather rarely and prefers to keep the term "love" for relations to those whom it will effectively reach and who will return it—fellow Christians. The Synoptic Gospels themselves present love of enemies not as the ideal kind of love but as the most certain expression of it (since there is nothing in enemies to motivate a natural love, which might then be mistaken for authentic Christian charity).

On the other hand, God's love goes out to the world (John 3:16), and Christians' love only reflects and shares in his. The universalist mission of Jesus to the world is passed on to the Church in John (15:27; 17:18; 20:21-23), and this is surely the Church's continuation of Jesus' mission of salvation in John 3:17, which is the manifestation of his Father's love (3:16). In limiting himself to a description of love of others as a mutual or fraternal love, John speaks of the fullest and most perfect realization of love that we have from Christ—a love that binds us together and to him because it is a share in the love that binds him and his Father together.

This brings us to Jesus' great prayer at the start of the passion in John 17, in which he explains the meaning and purpose of his redemptive incarnation (and he explains them in terms of love) and in which he asks the Father that this meaning be realized and this purpose accomplished. He notes that the hour of the great and full manifestation of his and the Father's glory or identity is at hand (verse 1). This manifestation—or communication—of divine glory will mean life for men, the life that consists in "knowledge," or experience, of God (verses 2-3). He explains that his whole ministry has been the communication of the Father's "name" (verse 6), "words" (verses 8 and 14), and "glory" (verse 22) to the disciples, who accepted this communication by their faith (verses 7-8). This resulted in their sharing in his mission (verse 18) and his joy (verse 13). Now he completes the divine self-communication by making himself "holy," that is, setting himself apart by passing from the world, so that they may be "made holy" too in perfect union with the "holy Father" (verses 11-19). But this "holiness" or union with the

Father consists (or shows itself) in the disciples' mutual union, which resembles the union of Father and Son (verse 11). It is this perfect union of all in and with Christ and through him with the Father that will demonstrate to the world the truth of Jesus' mission (verses 21-23). It will show the world that the Father loves them as he has loved the Son—that is, that the Father has communicated to the believers the divine reality, which the Father is and which is love, which he communicated to the Son in that he loved him before the world came to be and which is in the disciples because the Son is in them (verses 24-26).

Summary. We have, therefore, in the Johannine writings the following schema. The Father loves the Son and commands him to love us and thus to manifest his (the Father's) love for us. The Son in loving us both manifests to us the Father's love for us and loves the Father in return, thus establishing himself in the Father's love; the Son loves us (with a love that is the manifestation of the Father's love for us) and commands us to love one another after his example and thus to establish ourselves in his love; in loving one another, we love him (Christ) in return, and in this way we manifest to one another and to the whole world his (the Son's) love for men; in loving him in this way, we love the Father.

THE LOVE OPPOSED TO CHARITY

The Father loves the Son. He loves us in Christ. That is, he both loves us as Christ's disciples or members and manifests his love in the love Christ shows us, especially in his passion and resurrection. Our response to God's initiative consists in faith, which means acceptance of God's offer of his love. This acceptance results in our living God's life of love and so manifesting the divine love to the world. Our love must be modeled on God's (that is, on Christ's), reaching out to all and forgetful of selfish interests.

Sin an evil love. Occasionally New Testament writers speak of an undesirable sort of love—of a love that blocks the love which a Christian is called to share in and manifest. For example according to Luke 11:43 the Pharisees love the first places in the synagogues and greetings in the marketplaces (see also 20:46 and Matthew 23:6). According to 2 Timothy 4:10 Demas has forsaken the imprisoned Paul because he has "loved the present age." Or again, if we examine instances of the synonymous term "cherish," we find compound adjectives such as "cherishing money" rather frequently in descriptions of the evil and reprobate in the non-Johannine epistles. For example, in 2 Timothy 3:1-5 at the head of the list of the vices Paul sees rampant in the last days "cherishing self" and at the end "cherishing pleasure rather than cherishing God." Outside the Johannine writings, however, only rather disconnected mentions of undesirable love occur. In John and 1 John a rather clear image of this love appears. But we will be able to appreciate John's notion of the love opposed to charity better if we first examine in what terms the Synoptic Gospels and the Pauline epistles present the obstacle to Christian love and then against that background see how John explains this obstacle as an evil love.

God's plan was to give men a participation in his divine life of love through their union with his Son. However, to enjoy this participation, as we have already seen, it is not enough for a man simply to accept him as God's Son in human form. A renunciation is involved. Man as he is in the concrete must accept the Son of God as he became man in the concrete. But in the concrete man is sinful and Christ is a crucified Savior.

Sinful man is not disposed to accept a communication of the divine life, which is a life of love and which would raise him to the dignity of a child of God. Sin separates him from God, sets him in positive opposition to God, and tends to fix him definitively in this opposition in hell, or eternal death.

What is sin—that producer of death and sole obstacle to vital union with God? It is essentially a self-seeking on the Bible's own testimony. That type of all sin, the first, was nothing other than self-seeking or self-assertion: man's attempt to gain a coveted good independently of God and even against his plans—an attempt that resulted only in man's experience of his own vileness and inability to have anything apart from God (Genesis 3:1-7). Every sin is merely another act of this same self-assertion or self-seeking: the self-will of disobedience or stubbornness, the self-glorification of pride or vanity, the self-esteem of complacency, the self-indulgence of sensuality or sloth, the selfishness of avarice and greed. It is merely another act of that same self-seeking and like the first sin necessarily implies an opposition to God's plans and consequently also disregard for others (since his plan involves their good). All men are sinners (Romans 3:23); therefore all are selfish.

The New Testament in its insistence on humility, detachment, and self-renunciation as the indispensable conditions for union with Christ implies that the nature of sin is self-seeking. In the Gospels, for example, a man can save himself only by losing himself (Matthew 10:39; 16:25; Mark 8:35; Luke 9:24; 17:33; John 12:25).

Even more, the New Testament implies that sin is self-*love*. In the Synoptics Jesus not only insists that the disciples renounce themselves and carry the cross after him (Matthew 10:38; 16:24; Mark 8:34; Luke 9:23; 14:27). He demands further that they love him more than themselves; he even demands that they "hate" themselves to love him (Luke 14:26; Matthew 10:37). Often humility and abnegation recur as conditions for charity towards others: we must, for example, spend ourselves on and for others to the point of laying down our lives (Matthew 20:26-28; 23:11; Mark 9:35; 10:43-45; Luke 22:26-27). In fact, the most evidently authentic love is that in which personal interests are neglected or suffer most extensively—such as the love of persecutors (Matthew 5:44-48; Luke 6:27-36) or the love of the Good Samaritan (Luke 10:29-37).

For Paul humility—that is, practical recognition of the lowly place that belongs to us—regularly goes hand in hand with love and is often enough presented as the necessary condition for it. In Colossians 3:12 and Ephesians 4:2, for example, this humility enables the Christian's love to forgive injuries received (reminding the forgiver that he himself has received forgiveness from God). In Philippians 2:1-4 Paul's addressees will be like-minded and bound together by a unifying love only if they lay aside personal ambitions and humbly consider their fellows as their superiors.

For John, more clearly, the obstacle to faith mentioned repeatedly in the first half of his Gospel and the obstacle to charity mentioned in both the Gospel and the first epistle is love—an evil sort of love.

Faith finds itself countered by love. In John 3:16-21 those who refuse to believe or to come to the light (which is Christ) are those who love the darkness, that is, the evil works they do independently of God. In 12:37-43 the reason many have for not professing faith in Jesus is their love for the glory of men rather than the glory of God—that is, their preference for the glory and honor men give them over the glory they would give God and have from God by acknowledging the self-revelation God makes in Jesus. In 5:37-44 it is because they wish to receive glory from one another that they cannot submit to God by faith in his word, which Jesus speaks.

Love too finds itself impeded by another sort of love. In John 5:37-44 seeking glory from one another not only keeps Jesus' hearers from faith; it also explains why they do not have "the love of God" within them. In 1 John 2:15-16 a solemn warning against love of the world underscores the impossibility of a man's loving the world and at the same time having "the love of the Father" within him. "Do not love the world or what is in the world. If anyone loves the world, the love of the Father is not in him. For all that is in the world—the longing of the flesh and the longing of the eyes and the haughty airs of material well-being—is not from the Father but from the world." We have already seen that "the love of God" or "of the Father" may mean love for God but may also, and with some likelihood, mean God's own love which we share in as Christians. What excludes this "love of God" from a man's life is his giving in to his longing for the satisfaction of his fallen powers, his longing for possessions, and his haughtiness at being better off than others—in brief, his attachment to the values of the world that is opposed to God, his love for the selfish satisfaction it offers.

The tragedy of this clinging to what a man has independently of God lies in the fact that it leads to his destruction. A man's cherishing the life he has in this world ends in his losing it; only by "hating" the life he has in this world can he preserve himself for life of the coming age (John 12:25).

Undoing this evil love. Against the background of this appreciation of sin as a love opposed to the love Christ came to communicate to us, let us examine the New Testament conception of redemption and see if it cannot be understood in terms of love.

By sin man seeks his good or happiness apart from God, in whom alone as a creature he can find it (Genesis 2-3). He sets himself up as his own end, abandoning God, no longer ordering himself to God. It is easy to see that this idolatry of self necessarily excludes union with God and opposes man to God. It is also evident why man corrupted by sin, turned and ordered to self instead of being turned and ordered to God, can accept a share in God's life of selfless love only at the price of a painful renunciation of selfish love. Thus a fallen man's love necessarily costs him painful effort, quite differently from God's own love. But Christ's love cost him pain too because he became man like us: he came "in the likeness of sinful flesh" (Romans 8:3).

It is a human nature wounded by sin, even fallen under the dominion of sin (Romans 3:9-23), that the Son of God has come to save. He did this by assuming it just as he found it, marked with the stigma of sin, becoming like us in all things except guilt (Hebrews 2:17; 4:15) in order to make us like himself by elevating us to the dignity of sons of God (see 2 Corinthians 5:21: "Him who did not know sin God made sin, so that in him we might become the righteousness of God"). This passage from selfishness to love (since sin is selfishness and God's life is love) supposes a death to all that is selfish in us. It is a passage which sinful man, deprived of God's support and set in opposition to him, cannot accomplish for himself. Hence the role of Christ's cross, that mystery of renunciation, in the divine plan of salvation.

In the Synoptics Jesus presents his passion as a condition he must fulfill if he is to attain his glory: he had to suffer and enter his glory (Luke 24:26; see also 9:31). So too, the disciples are not merely going to share in Jesus' glory; they must carry the cross afer him and drink from his cup as necessary conditions (Matthew 20:22-23; Mark 10:38-39; and see the references to cross-carrying given on pages 81 and 82.

If the cross is a necessary condition for glory in the first three Gospels, it also seems to be a necessary condition for charity. According to the Synoptics the cross is the great expression of Christ's love for men: he has come to serve and to give his life as a ransom for many (Matthew 20:28; Mark 10:45; Luke 22:27). His disciples must certainly imitate him by serving one another—even, it seems implied, to the point of laying down their lives for one another.

The Synoptics do not explain the reason for the necessary connection between the cross and glory. Neither do they explain why a true charity is so costly to the person who loves.

The fourth Gospel and the Johannine epistles are somewhat more explicit. Jesus' passion and resurrection constitute his passage (or passover) from this world to the Father (John 13:1). He accomplishes it so that his disciples can follow him: he is only going to prepare a place for them and will return to take them to himself (14:2-3). He wants them to be where he is, and this is possible only if they follow him (12:26). Such following means being different, being set aside from the world, or being "sanctified" as he "sanctified" or separated himself from the world by his passion-resurrection (17:15-19). This "passage" or "sanctification" or "glorification" of Jesus gives him the "glory" which belongs to him as Son of God (17:5). But why it must be painful is not clear—why it must mean dying like the grain of wheat (12:25), why it must be an experience so fearful that Jesus at first draws back from it (12:27-28). That this painful experience is a manifestation of love is, of course, explicit, as we have already seen—the great expression of Jesus' love for the Father (14:31) and for his disciples (15:13; 13:1). And the disciples must love with the same sort of painful love, readily giving even their lives for one another (1 John 3:16; John 15:12-13). We are left to conclude for ourselves that the painfulness of the process comes from the fact that the world of fallen man from which we must break away is a world of selfish love or attachment to the things that fallen man has independently of God.

In order to enter into the state which befits and belongs to the Son of God, the man Jesus had, for Paul too, to pass definitively from the world of sin by the self-renunciation of his passion and resurrection. "The death he died, he died once and for all to sin; the life he lives, he lives for God" (Romans 6:10). He passed completely beyond the dominion of death (6:9) to a life dominated by the Father's glory (6:4). Paul even says that Jesus became Son of God by reason of his (passion and) resurrection (Romans 1:4; see also Acts 13:33). Not that God was not his Father until then, but only then did the man Jesus enter into that state which belonged to him as Son: a state of glory or of manifestly divine life, impossible as long as he remained in the world of sin. The several statements in Acts that Jesus is messiah and savior (2:36; 5:30-31) or giver of blessings (3:26) because he is risen must be understood in the same way as these Pauline statements: only when he has entered into glory, only when he has begun to live a life lived completely for the Father without any of the effects of sin operative in it, do we have a life in which to share. For our life is a share in his. With him we have been crucified to the world (Galatians 6:14). With him we have died, are risen, and therefore are living (Romans 6:3-11; Galatians 2:19-20; Ephesians 2:5-6; Colossians, 1:14,20; 2:20; 3:1-4; see also Philippians 3:10-11). He died that we might live for him (Romans 14:7-9; 2 Corinthians 5:15).

Christ is the head of a redeemed humanity. He became man only to enable the whole of fallen mankind to share in his own dignity as Son. "He was handed over for *our* transgressions and rose for *our* justification" (Romans 4:25). The passion and the resurrection of Christ are the means by which *we* in our turn can pass from the state of sinful men to the divine life of sons. But we must use this means. For the glory of Christ to become a reality for us, it is necessary that his cross become a reality in our lives. To share in the glory of Christ, we must also share in his cross. To live the divine life we must pass with him, our head, from the world of sin. "We will be glorified with him," Paul writes, "provided that we suffer with him too" (Romans 8:17).

But this passage by suffering is not accomplished in a single act. Our whole Christian life is a progressive realization in ourselves of the double mystery of cross and resurrection, of renunciation and life. Though already from baptism we must consider ourselves as "dead to sin and as living for God in Christ," sin can still regain control (Romans 6:11-13). Even more, the effects of sin (concupiscence, suffering, death) still have some place in our life, and we need to be ever occupied putting to death what Paul calls our "earthly members" (Colossians 3:5; see also Romans 8:13; 1 Corinthians 9:27), that is, the selfish tendencies of our not yet wholly redeemed selves (Romans 8:23). We must be incessantly struggling to root selfishness ever more completely out of our lives. But our celebration of the Eucharist is our most effective sharing in Christ's paschal act (1 Corinthians 11).

The final step is the renunciation which Paul calls being set free to be with the Lord (Philippians 1:23). The complete sharing that awaits those who have taken the final step is final resurrection, when at the return of Christ all things will be put under his feet and death, the last enemy of God's plan to be done away with, is destroyed by the resurrection of the dead and God becomes everything for everyone (1 Corinthians 15:20-28; 1 Thessalonians 4:14).

If for Paul, as we have seen above, Jesus' death is the great manifestation of love and if it is our task as those who are "in Christ" to grow in love, may we not rightly consider the Christian's progressive death to sin a progressive death to selfishness or self-love and his progressive sharing in Christ's life a progressive sharing in a life which is love?

For Paul, then, as well as for John, Christ's work of redemption (and our lifelong work of sharing in his paschal mystery) is a matter of passing effectively and completely from the domination of self-love to a life of charity, which is the life of God.

Summary. Sin is the one obstacle to God's plans. New Testament authors often describe specific sins as an evil sort of love—love of money, pleasure, and the like. The Johannine writings suggest that all sin is a particular sort of evil love: self-love.

Already in Genesis 3 sin appears as self-seeking and self-assertion. The New Testament implies that sin is self-seeking by insisting on the need for self-renunciation as the condition for union with Christ. Even more, the Synoptics indicate that love for Jesus excludes a certain love of self. The Pauline epistles too make it clear that a Christian can love only if he is ready to renounce himself. John points out that this renunciation of self needed before a man will accept Christ by faith and live God's life of love is a repudiation of self-love—a love for what a man has independently of God.

Christ came into a selfish world in order to pass from it by his passion to a life lived for the Father. He did this for us so that we could make the passage with him. It is a passage from the world of sin—that is, self-love—to a divine life—that is, a life of charity. Our whole Christian life from its start at baptism through its repeated struggles and especially its frequent Eucharistic celebrations to its consummation at the final resurrection is a progressive sharing in this paschal mystery of Christ—this mystery of renouncing self-love in order to share more and more fully in the charity that is God's life.

THE CHARACTERISTICS OF CHRISTIAN LOVE

Now that we have completed our examination of New Testament teaching on love, we may describe this love that constitutes the core of Christianity as the passages considered present it.

The *agápē*—love of God for men (especially for his Son and for Christians), of man for God (and Christ), and of the Christian for his neighbor—is always and everywhere a disinterested and efficacious benevolence. These three aspects—benevolence, disinterestedness, efficacy—stand out as love's most obvious characteristics and can help us to understand the others.

The charity of God or of the Christian is always a benevolence since it always seeks the good of the person loved and rejoices in that good.

It is disinterested since it not only does not seek its own advantage but rather disregards it or even renounces it for the good of the person loved. Thus God loves men and does not spare his only Son (Romans 8:32); Christ loves them and gives his life for them (for example, Romans 8:34; Ephesians 5:2; John 10:10-11; 15:13); and Christians must also be ready to give their lives for their neighbors (for example, John 15:12; 1 John 3:16).

Finally, charity is an efficacious benevolence since it is not content to remain a simple affection but always expresses itself in action on behalf of the one loved (see 1 John 3:16-18; James 2:8-16; 1 Corinthians 13). This is true even in the extreme cases of love for persecutors and love for God. Love of persecutors expresses itself at least in prayers offered for them (Matthew 5:44; Luke 6:27-28), and love for God (to whom creatures can hardly do good) is shown by acts of obedience—an obedience to the command to love like him, and therefore by acts which manifest his love to the world (John 15:10; 14:31; 17:21-23).

Two further characteristics deserve attention. First, universality. Christian love excludes no one but extends even to the wicked and persecutors (Matthew 5:44; Luke 6:27). This universality of charity is connected, it would seem, with its disinterestedness. Since it is without self-seeking, it has no reason to limit itself to those in whom it finds some utility or to whom some personal attachment binds it.

Finally, charity is of itself reciprocal or mutual. This does not mean that it loves only those who love in return. But the New Testament authors do not speak of those who refuse the benevolence offered them (those, for example, who refuse the offer of conversion to Christ or those who respond to the benevolence of Christians with persecutions and insults) in the same way in which it speaks of those who accept.

The conception of love as an efficacious benevolence seems to be why the term most often designates the love of God for Christians (those who love him in return) and the benevolence of Christians for one another (mutual or fraternal charity). The certain cases where the New Testament inculcates or praises love for those who are clearly not followers of Christ are rare: the Synoptics do so in their passages on the love of persecutors in the Sermon on the Mount and in the parable of the Good Samaritan, Paul perhaps twice (Romans 13:8 and 1 Thessalonians 3:12), John never. When there is question of God's love for the world or for sinners, it is a love conditioned by man's acceptance (for example, his love for the world in John 3:16) or one whose success in achieving its benevolent designs is taken for granted (for example, his love for sinners in Romans 5:8). Those who accept the love offered them are simply and fully "loved."

If an occasional text insists on the Christian's love of enemies to emphasize the universality of charity, none makes of such love the most typical example of charity. (Matthew 5:44 and Luke 6:27 inculcate a love which extends *even* to one's enemies—see Matthew 5:47: "If you love *only* your brothers"—

that is, the universality of charity—love of enemies, those with whom we have the least bonds or ties, being the ideal instance for illustrating this universality.) As a matter of fact, passages on love of enemies are rare (and even those on benevolence towards enemies are not frequent), and texts on love for the devils or the damned are simply nonexistent.

The New Testament writers seem hesitant to designate as love a benevolence which is manifested towards those who will refuse it—almost as if it could be called love only in a less strict, less exact sense of the word. The reason for this seems to be that for the New Testament true, full charity is a reciprocal love. This reciprocity seems bound up with the efficacy of Christian love. Love that is accepted—that succeeds in doing the good that it intends—is efficacious. Love that is refused—that tries in vain to realize its aims—remains ineffective in some sense—though in another it may be considered effective: that is, insofar as it expresses itself in (unsuccessful) action. But *agápē* is an efficacious love.

Nevertheless, as long as the persons who refuse the good one wishes to do them are not yet irrevocably fixed in their destiny, there always remains the possibility for love to attain the end it intends. Occasionally, therefore, we find mention of love for them before this decisive moment, but never for the damned. If of itself charity knows no limits, those who are its objects can refuse its advances and even exclude themselves definitively from all possibility of profiting by it.

Christian love, then, is a benevolence both disinterested and efficacious and therefore universal and reciprocal. It is this love that is God's own life and which he communicates to men in the crucified and risen Christ.

RÉSUMÉ

God is love. All that he manifests to us of his intimate divine life is that it is a life of disinterested and efficacious love. He manifests this in his incarnate Son, especially in what Christ does in suffering and rising for us. But this deed of Christ is not merely a manifestation of divine love; it is an offer to men of a share in the divine life of love. If men will accept union with the Son by reception of the Son's Spirit, they will become objects of the Father's love for his Son.

Man responds to God's offer by faith. By faith he accepts Christ as the offer which divine love makes of itself: by his faith he believes in God as love, submits to the domination of divine love over his life.

From this acceptance on man's part results the new, divine life he leads—a life of love. Fraternal charity is the infallible manifestation of this divine life in us; become sons of God, we resemble our Father, live his life, share in his divine life by showing authentic, unselfish love for our neighbor.

If fraternal charity is the presence and real expression of the divine life in Christians, it is easy to understand why it is the great—indeed the only—

permanent visible manifestation of the divine love (and in this sense the only permanent tangible presence of God) in the world today. God showed the depth and immensity of his love in sending his Son "so that we might live by him" (1 John 4:9). The Son by fulfilling his mission—in other words, by working for our good or by loving us—has shown (and offered) us the love of the Father. Today Christ is no longer visibly present among us. Only the eyes of faith can discern him in the Eucharist or in the events his providence disposes. But his disciples and they alone—his Church, his members still in the world, the visible branches attached to the invisible vine and living its life—by their life of charity present to the world in a tangible way the God who is love.

The neighbor whom we love is one with Christ and Christ is one with the Father. Hence, our love for neighbor is ultimately love for Christ and for God. Charity, then, is not only God's love within us but also love for God.

It is this charity that is the vital force which animates the Church—ideally a community of charity according to the description given by Acts 2:42-47 and 4:32-35, although the word "love" does not occur. Coming as it does from the depths of the Trinity, ceaselessly diffusing itself and growing within the Christian community, it returns ultimately, in spending itself on the neighbor who is one with Christ, to the source from which it came.

The only obstacle to the development of this divine life is sin, which is selfishness or self-love. To free ourselves more and more of sin and all its effects—to pass from this world of sin—we must from the moment of our baptism share more and more fully in that act of total self-renunciation which was the cross of Christ. We thereby share more and more fully in his glory until by our final resurrection we pass to that plenitude of divine life in which neither the selfishness of sin nor any of its effects can have part: a life where God is everything for everyone, a life which is nothing but love.

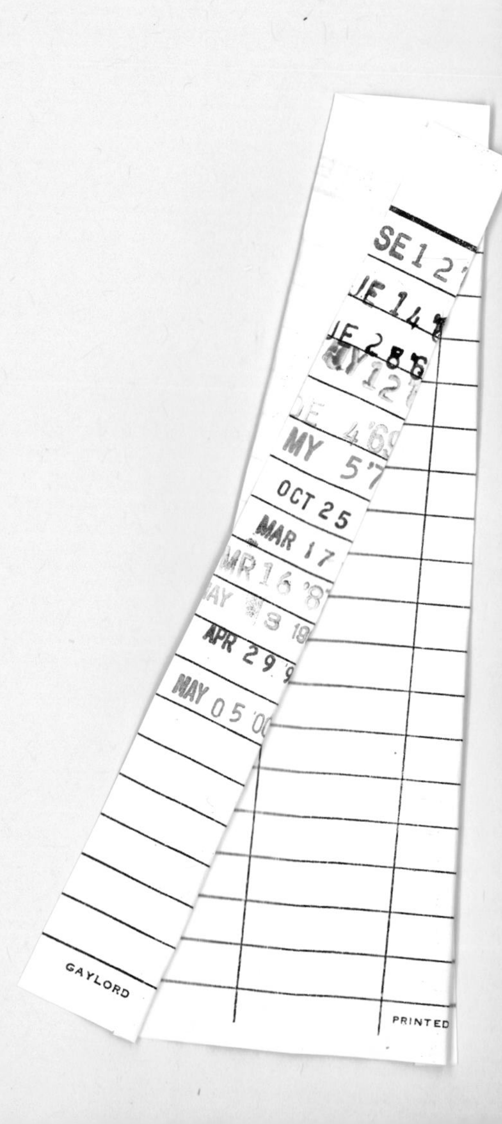
SE 1 2
JE 14
JE 28
MY 12
DE 4 '69
MY 5 '7
OCT 25
MAR 17
MR 16 '8
MAY 3 19
APR 29 '9
MAY 05 '00
GAYLORD
PRINTED